LEARNING TO PLAY BY EAR
ESSAYS AND EARLY POEMS
by Lisel Mueller

Juniper Press
La Crosse, WI
1990

W.N.J. Series, number 26
(cloth) ISBN 1-55780-137-1 / $20.00
(paper) ISBN 1-55780-138-X / $12.00

ACKNOWLEDGEMENTS

The twenty-four poems appearing here were taken from the volume Dependencies, published in 1965 by the University of North Carolina Press.

"Learning to Play by Ear" was first published by Two Hands Press, Chicago, 1980.

"Return" is reprinted from New Letters, volume 52,2-3, winter/spring 1986.

"Two Strains: Some Thoughts About English Words" was first published in Ploughshares, volume 5, number 1.

"'After Whistler': A Poem in Search of Itself" was first published in The Brockport Forum, SUNY Brockport, 1982.

"An Interview with Lisel Mueller" first appeared in AWP Newsletter, September 1984, and was reprinted in Finding the Words, Interviews with Writers Who Teach, by Nancy Bunge, published by Swallow/Ohio University Press, 1985.

Cover drawing by Terry Valley

TABLE OF CONTENTS

THE BLIND LEADING THE BLIND

Take my hand. There are two of us in this cave.
The sound you hear is water; you will hear it forever.
The ground you walk on is rock. I have been here before.
People come here to be born, to discover, to kiss,
to dream and to dig and to kill. Watch for the mud.
Summer blows in with scent of horses and roses;
fall with the sound of sound breaking; winter shoves
its empty sleeve down the dark of your throat.
You will learn toads from diamonds, the fist from the palm,
love from the sweat of love, falling from flying.
There are a thousand turnoffs. I have been here before.
Once I fell off a precipice. Once I found gold.
Once I stumbled on murder, the thin parts of a girl.
Walk on, keep walking, there are axes above us.
Watch for occasional bits and bubbles of light--
birthdays for you, recognitions: <u>yourself,</u> <u>another.</u>
Watch for the mud. Listen for bells, for beggars.
Something with wings went crazy against my chest once.
There are two of us here. Touch me.

IN THE THRIVING SEASON
In memory of my mother

Now as she catches fistfuls of sun
riding down dust and air to her crib,
my first child in her first spring
stretches bare hands back to your darkness
and heals your silence, the vast hurt
of your deaf ear and mute tongue
with doves hatched in her young throat.

Now ghost-begotten infancies
are the marrow of trees and pools
and blue uprisings in the woods
spread revolution to the mind,
I can believe birth is fathered
by death, believe that she was quick
when you forgave pain and terror
and shook the fever from your blood.

Now in the thriving season of love
when the bud relents into flower,
your love turned absence has turned once more,
and if my comforts fall soft as rain
on her flutters, it is because
love grows by what it remembers of love.

BACH TRANSCRIBING VIVALDI

One remembered the sunrise, how clearly it gave
substance and praise to the mountains of the world;
the other imagined twilight, the setting in blood,
and a valley of fallen leaves where a stranger might rest.

One avoided the forest and made his way through fields
where the sky was constant and clouds rang in his ears;
the other cut through the thicket, the thorns and vines
and was not touched, except by the dying of men.

One asked the road to the land of the golden lion
whose eyes never weep, whose lifted hand scepters
the seasons of stars and the grafting of generations;
the other searched for the kingdom of the lamb
with the trembling fleece, whose live unreasoning heart
consumes the mortal treasure of his loves.

Still, at one point of the journey one must have seen
the afternoon dip and drop away into shade
and the other come to a place where the forest cleared
into white and violet patches of stars.

"MORE LIGHT"
(Words attributed to Goethe on his deathbed)
    For my father

He, too, went down on occasion,
touched land on the pitch-black bottom
of fish that can do without eyes,
tangled with spiny and slimy life,
with creatures all greedy feelers,
all sting, strike, suction,
unknown to moonlight. There must have been times
when there seemed no end to coral gardens
and the imperturbable waving of sea fans
while clamor he had not thought possible
pressed on his eardrums its rhythms
of rancorless lust. To think,
when he pleasure-sailed on the Adriatic
--August afternoons--
atop a mirror that gave of nothing
but his sure, shaved face
and an indestructible sky,
how thin that surface, how impudent!
Salons, of course, and claret and ladies with taste;
walks and sonatas and careful conversations
that could be printed verbatim;
unflinching eyes and a statesman's profile:
but there was restless Werther
and hell-bent, curious Faust.
He must have been there, gone back
to explore the secret canals
of succulent sponges, to drift
by the faint luminescence of stripes,
to let his conscience slip off

in the subtleties of the dark.
But always the clean, sharp hurt
of remembered sunlight pulled him
clear of a mermaid's breast
toward a place where men try to prove
by courtesy and equations
and by occasional mercy
that there are lovelier creatures
and more delicate pearls.

NINE MONTHS MAKING

Nine months making
the pulse and tissue of love
work knowledge upon us;
the hard squeeze against bone
makes radical trial
of love's primal claim:
here in the body truth grows palpable.

Long comprehended, never
till now understood, the ancient analogy
of sap in the root as impulse
toward flowering, as drive and push
toward all possibility,
is proven upon us. Mind
tried and failed; it is body
secretes the slow-spun pearl
we say is knowledge, oystered
in our infinitely expanding
one-man and one-woman world.

Knowledge of act, not cause.
Love's wine has been our blood
for years; we shall not know
what word or weather thickened
the familiar flux, quickened
old essence into separateness of flesh.
Change and astonishment
witnessed upon my body and your eyes
these long fall evenings
unhand the shape, not mystery, of love.

Nor need we know
more than these sweetly growing pains
which are enough to publish
love's increasing refusal
to lie with the biblical dust of our bones.

THE POWER OF MUSIC TO DISTURB

A humid night. Mad June bugs dash themselves
against a window they should know is there;
I hear an owl awaking in the woods
behind our house, and wonder if it shakes
sleep from its eyes and lets its talons play,
stretch and retract, rehearsing for the kill--
and on the radio the music drives
toward death by love, for love, because of love
like some black wave that cannot break itself.

It is a music that luxuriates
in the impossibilities of love
and rides frustration till two ghosts become
alive again, aware of how the end
of every act of love is separateness;
raw, ruthless lovers, desperate enough
to bank on the absurdity of death
for royal consummation, permanence
of feeling, having, knowing, holding on.

My God, he was a devil of a man
who wrote this music so voluptuous
it sucks me in with possibilities
of sense and soul, of pity and desire
which place and time make ludicrous: I sit
across from you here in our living room
with chairs and books and red geraniums
and ordinary lamplight on the floor
after an ordinary day of love.

How can disaster be so beautiful?
I range the beaches of our lucid world
against that flood, trying to think about
our child upstairs, asleep with her light on
to keep her from vague evils; about us
whose loving has become so natural
that is has rid itself of teeth and claws,

implements for the lovers new at love,
whose jitters goad them into drawing blood.

But o my love, I cannot beat it back,
neither the sound nor what the sound lets loose;
the opulence of agony drowns out
the hard, dry smack of death against the glass
and batters down the sea walls of my mind,
and I am pulled to levels below light
where easy ways of love are meaningless
and creatures feel their way along the dark
by shock of ecstasy and heat of pain.

ON FINDING A BIRD'S BONES IN THE WOODS

Even Einstein, gazing
at the slender ribs of the world,
examining and praising
the cool and tranquil core
under the boil and burning
of faith and metaphor--
even he, unlearning
the bag and baggage of notion,
must have kept some shred
in which to clothe that shape,
as we, who cannot escape
imagination, swaddle
this tiny world of bone
in all that we have known
of sound and motion.

CICADAS

Always in unison, they are
the rapt voice of silence,

so singleminded I cannot tell
if the sound is rich or thin,

cannot tell even if it is sound,
the high, sustained note

which gives to a summer field
involved with the sun at noon

a stillness as palpable
as smoke and mildew,

know only: when they are gone
one scrubbed autumn day

after the clean sweep
of the bright, acrid season,

what remains is a clearing of rest,
of balance and attention

but not the second skin,
hot and close, of silence.

THE MERMAID

All day he had felt her stirring
under the boat, and several times
when the net had tightened, frog-nervous,
he had bungled the pulling-in,
half-glad of the stupid, open mouths
he could throw back.
At sundown
the shifting and holding of time and air
had brought her to the still surface,
to sun herself in the last, slow light
where lilies and leeches tangled and rocked.
He could have taken her then, aimed his net
as dragonfly hunters do when the glassy gliding
of rainbows goes to their heads,
could have carried her home on tiptoe
and lifted her lightly, ever so lightly,
over his sill.
      And, hopeless, knew
that to have her alive was only this:
the sounding, casting, waiting, seeing
and praying the light not to move,
not yet to round the bay of her shoulder
and passing, release her
to the darkness he would not enter.

MOON FISHING

When the moon was full they came to the water,
some with pitchforks, some with rakes,
some with sieves and ladles
and one with a silver cup.

And they fished till a traveler passed them and said,
"Fools,
to catch the moon you must let your women
spread their hair on the water--
even the wily moon will leap to that bobbing
net of shimmering threads,
gasp and flop till its silver scales
lie black and still at your feet."

And they fished with the hair of their women
till a traveler passed them and said,
"Fools,
do you think the moon is caught lightly,
with glitter and silk threads?
You must cut our your hearts and bait your hooks
with those dark animals;
what matter you lose your hearts to reel in your dream?"

And they fished with their tight, hot hearts
till a traveler passed them and said,
"Fools,
what good is the moon to a heartless man?
Put back your hearts and get on your knees
and drink as you never have,
until your throats are coated with silver
and your voices ring like bells."

And they fished with their lips and tongues
until the water was gone
and the moon had slipped away
in the soft, bottomless mud.

SANS SOUCI
(Frederick the Great's summer palace near Potsdam)

It does not make sense in terms of historical fact,
the unabashed gesture, the celebration of joy,
birds that catch and diffract
the afternoon sun and drink from a bubbling nymph
who beckons a marble boy;

nor the make-believe heaven inside: golden frames
looping their spiraling curls about mirrors that blaze
whirlpools of light on the games
of Arcadian lovers dappling a celadon wall;
yet we might have expected it. Praise

is the louder and passion the fiercer for need,
fiercest when bred in a mind that has knelt to a whip
and recanted its natural creed
of splendor and bliss. Rigidity once removed
is freedom and grace, and the tight-stretched line of a lip

curves to the flute's convolutions of silver and breath.
But for the hair that we split in order to prove
otherwise, death
reverses to motion and sunlight. Turned inside-out,
negation is equal to love.

A GRACKLE OBSERVED

Watching the black grackle
come out of the gray shade
into the sun, I am dazzled
by an unsuspected sheen,
yellow, purple, and green,
where the comb of light silkens
unspectacular wings--
until he, unaware
of what he means at this one
peculiar angle of sun,
hops back to his modest dark
and leaves the shining part
of himself behind, as though
brightness must outgrow
its fluttering worldly dress
and enter the mind outright
as vision, as pure light.

THE LONESOME DREAM

In the America of the dream
the first rise of the moon
swings free of the ocean,
and she reigns in her shining flesh
over a good, great valley
of plumed, untrampled grasses
and beasts with solemn eyes,
of lovers infallibly pitched
in their ascendant phase.

In this America, death
is virginal also, roaming
the good, great valley
in his huge boots, his shadow
steady and lean, his pistol
silver, his greeting clear
and courteous as a stranger's
who looks for another, a mind
to share his peaceable evenings.

Dreaming, we are another
race than the one which wakes
in the cold sweat of fear,
fires wild shots at death,
builds slippery towers of glass
to head him off, waylays him
with alcohol traps, rides him down
in the haunts of thought and thighs,
our teetering ghost towns.

Dreaming, we are the mad
who swear by the blood of trees
and speak with the tongues of streams
through props of steel and sawdust;

a colony of souls
ravaged by visions, bound
to some wild, secret cove
not yet possessed, a place
still innocent of us.

FIGURE FOR A LANDSCAPE

Look, the solitary walker
out on this coldest Sunday of the year
shoulders the whole burden of the fable
which winter is, the moral panorama
of a silence so vast that all sounds have meaning.

In summer the landscape was simply
itself, and concealment humanly possible
in grass and shadow and the living noise
of child singers and animal dancers,
baroque in their cultivation of opulence

and the green life. But now
even the lake is petrified out of sound,
and the sky, impartially plundered
of inessential leaves, birds, clouds,
throws back his face without kindly distortion

as though he alone could answer for winter.
The tracks of the dead and the dying accost him,
crossing his footprints wherever he walks,
stands, is alive; and the clamor of ice
comes down with a crash, like an unstruck bell,

splitting his ears. In this season,
while we stay home with coffee and morning
newspapers, sensible of the danger
confronting us in the sight of a branch
gloved by a child's lost mitten,

he is the hero who bears all loss,
who, by no particular virtue
other than solitude, takes on himself
the full silence, the whole terrible
knowledge the landscape no longer conceals.

THE BRIDE'S COMPLAINT

I saw the face of my love naked
and that was more than my love could bear--
o red-eyed bull of the sun,
how many times must I cross you?

My kisses are petals past his mouth
and sparrows twitter away my breath--
whirligig world, run slow, run down,
let my love remember me!

FIRST SNOW IN LAKE COUNTY

All night it fell around us
as if the sky had been sheared,
its fleece dropping forever
past our windows, until our room
was as chaste and sheltered
as Ursula's, where she lay
and dreamed herself in heaven:
and in the morning we saw
that the vision had held, looked out
on such a sight as we wish for
all our lives:
a thing, place, time
untouched and uncorrupted,
the world before we were here.

Even the wind held its peace.

And already, as our eyes
hung on, hung on, we longed
to make that patience bear
our tracks, already our daughter
put on her boots and screamed,
and the dog jumped with the joy
of splashing the white with yellow
and digging through the snow
to the scents and sounds below.

AFTERTHOUGHTS ON THE LOVERS

I imagine them always in summer,
with roses running a loose-lipped hazard
around their book, as butterflies
poised in the net of noon:
I think of her silent, wholly brought
under siege by his voice, staring
confusion down to the marble squares,
hearing and trying not to hear
how sweetly Lancelot plagued the queen.

What if they had outlived
their full-bloom summer, had dwindled
into the blight of autumn
and trees shedding their leaves
had brought them dreams, such dreams--
if mind on the prowl for flesh
had set its teeth on love
and pointed fingers at their furtiveness?

What if no violence
had sealed their immortality
for us, who need to think of love
as a fixed sun, impervious to our passing
in and out of the shade?

SUSPENSION BRIDGE: TWILIGHT

The smoking, rusting beast
--our green ankylosaurus--

refines itself to a hum
between these silver strands

hammered for an imagined
woman's white-knuckled wrist

--a lady's rather, small,
slenderly old fashioned,

the wrist of one who delights
in such sherbet sunsets

as this one in raspberry, filched
from a romance. Yet we bump

ashore in another part
of the land, and looking back

see her stand unbroken,
swaying only a little

as if she felt, too late,
the weight of our bon voyage.

THE CREMONA VIOLIN
(After E.T.A. Hoffmann's story)

Two red spots on Antonia's cheeks
gave early warning. So her father-lover,
swearing that she should never
sing again, took down the violin
Amati or perhaps Guarneri made,
as proxy for her voice.

Evenings he played, doors shut to company.
Then her breath rose, eyes glistened, muscles tensed
until, fatigued, she took
a low bow and cried out,
"I never was better, father;
how well you make me sing!"

Priceless to him, those evenings with his daughter
whom neither the world nor another lover
should ever claim again.
Now that she was his instrument,
he learned new subtleties of playing,
new ways of tenderness.

And killed her with that playing. Her flawed chest
could not abide love's labor. When she died
he broke the singing body into bits,
and hung a cypress wreath
where it had been, and danced
a dance of death, his black crape flying.

THE MIDNIGHT CHILD

Then the moon threw pebbles
on the small boy's window
and took him past sleeping dogs
into the night of black roses
and small shivers of grass.

Into the shoreless night.
Through faceless wax daisies,
through clover, hint of honey
in the drained, bleached fields.
To the edge of the woods, and there
to wait in weeds and shadows.

His cheeks still warm with kisses.
And when the beast came out
between the trees, all hide,
all claws, all bloodshot eyes,
the child was not afraid.
And would have left that place
quiet and sure, until
he saw the beast slip off
his hairy skin, become
a gathering of whiteness
and small shivers of flesh,
a naked human shape
alone and ignorant
in a thin patch of light.

And then the cry, the child's
runaway voice, the heart
wild in the net of the moon.

NOLI ME TANGERE

Leave me, she said to me,
you will not find in my murdered flesh
a tooth or hair of death;
though you breathe into my mouth
with your incessant whys
I will not give death away.

You shall not twist my bones
into a star's shape, nor plant my hair
as roots for the dreams of the living;
and if you open my heart
and run your poet's fingers
over its walls and cushions
you will find it is like yours,
dark.

Leave me, she said,
said her slayer, said
the Negro boy in the river,
said the bureaucrat of the ovens,
said the millions in cattle graves,

leave us.

ECOLOGY: THE LION

Let me illustrate by way of example
from history, from the last war:
when the city burned that day, that night,
those many days and nights, the flames
finally bit through the bars of his cage
and set him free. He was wary of freedom
at first, of its charred, black taste. But the fire
drove him out of the zoo and eastward,
and his confidence grew in the burned-out streets
where children stuck to the boiling asphalt;
heat urged his soles like the native heat
of his rampant days, and when he reached
the river, spurred by sounds of panic
breaking through leafage of smoke,
he felt easy enough to stand still
and savor the scent of catastrophe
that welcomed him like a greeting from home.

IN MEMORY OF ANTON WEBERN, DEAD SEPTEMBER 15, 1945

"On leaving the house of his son-in-law in Mittersill, near Salzburg,
Anton Webern, 62-year-old Austrian composer of micromusically
subtilized instrumental works, is accidentally killed by an American
sentinel in consequence of his failure to obey a misinterpreted signal
to stop."

> Slonimsky, Music since 1900

Tinged leaves lie
on the Austrian earth, like scabs
closing wounds, and guns
are stacked with last summer's hay
in warm, dry places. Home
is again a room where a crackling fire
ripens late apples on the window sill
for a child's eventual pleasure:
so subtly does patience turn the years
and prove despair a changeling.
Women in shawls and men
with the simple minds of saints
stop at the wayside shrines
where Christ hangs dozenfold
from rusted nails, to gather
strength for the winter, as if
gathering armloads of fuel.
Yet he who coaxed
dissonant music out from behind those crude
crossings of common wood
is dead of the peace which made such intricate music
in his ears that night, is dead
of the deadly habit, is dead
of incomprehension, is dead.
May he rest easy in his fashion
of lightness, though the knuckle of our doubt
scrapes hard against his grave,
dredging his silence for the gold of purpose:
o there is hope that lambs of snow

may settle our wilderness
with the simple charity
of whiteness one of these autumn nights,
muffling our mouths out of questions
after the sense of things.

AN ANCIENT WOMAN

I knew an ancient woman once
across a passage of despair
whose eyes were full of clouds, whose hair
was part and parcel of the dance

of light across the flesh of grass,
who said, "The other side of death
is easier on blood and breath
but o the wilderness you cross!"

Who said, "The passage of despair
lies between coveting and not,
between I shall and I forgot,
between the object and the air
that runs through bone-dry hands like sea.
Child, child, you need an angel there," said she.

LEARNING TO PLAY BY EAR

    <u>Apprenticeship</u>: the word conjures up centuries of young men standing at the easel or the blacksmith's forge, in the tannery or the tailor shop, learning how to do something and do it well. It conjures up an older, or perhaps old, man, a master who believes in his craft and is proud of his professionalism, and who considers it a privilege to pass his knowledge on to a younger man. It has to do with tradition and with what we now call "standards," and what would perhaps have been called "honor" in the days of Hans Sachs, that master cobbler and master singer of Renaissance Nuremberg, who saw to it that the best man won the singing contest. It brings to mind a particular folktale, as told by the Brothers Grimm, whose hero has never known fear and sets out to learn what he has been missing. Like other young men he travels and finds master teachers who think they have sure-fire methods of scaring him. But of course it's no use; he appears to be unteachable. His experience with fear comes when he least expects it, but he instantly recognizes it as the real thing, and he shivers. Let's say he is the poet seized by the "shock of recognition;" he had to discover the deep-down mystery which no one could explain to him, and until he did all the techniques in the world were wasted on him.

    In this case the apprentice is a she, and she does not know where the impulse to transform feeling into form and language comes from. She is myself; and I am unusual among American poets only because the language I write in is my second language, thrust upon me at the age of fifteen, when I arrived in Evansville, Indiana from Nazi Germany. In retrospect, I think it was probably the best time for me to be forced to make the switch. At fifteen you want more than anything to be accepted, assimilated into the environment around you--the loathsome term "peer group" had not been invented--and though I was never to overcome my natural condition as a loner, the motivation to blend into the prevailing culture was strong, if not entirely conscious. Besides, I had to pass high school history and English courses. I had had some English in my German school. The system had dwelt heavily on grammar and spelling, which gave me a good base to start from, and seven hours of high school daily saw to it that I added to my vocabulary rapidly. I remember listening to the radio a lot in order to understand the accents of voices without faces.

I learned to understand speakers and announcers; the words sung by popular singers took longer. And even when I had every song on the "Hit Parade" down cold, there was the puzzle of metaphor. For a long time I did not make the connection between "a blanket of blue" and the sky, nor did I realize that the "deep purple" which falls (over sleepy garden walls) was the shadows of early evening.

Perhaps it was this initial inability to absorb metaphor in English that caused me to be left unimpressed by the poets we studied in high school English and American literature classes. But during my one year of high school a classmate introduced me to Carl Sandburg, and I was hooked. Most of the German poetry I knew had been from the 19th century, or else it was in the late romantic vein of the early 20th. Sandburg's unadorned, muscular, straightforward diction lured me as the painted women under the streetlamps lured the farm boys in a city named Chicago. It was my first encounter with a modern idiom in poetry, and it was the right one for me at this point, because it was not difficult. Literal yet evocative, I found it as exotic as the night train on which someone softly says, "Omaha."

Sandburg and adolescence conspired, and I started to write poems. Terrible poems. Cliches that came out of loneliness and daydreams. But without Sandburg I might not have found even a beginning. Later, in college, I fell in love with Keats. I took a course in modern American poetry and came under the spell of some of Conrad Aiken's short poems with their sensuous sound, their long, rhythmic lines. I also liked Robinson Jeffers and the impressionistic poems of John Gould Fletcher. All these poets had large reputations during the Forties and were amply represented in the Untermeyer anthology we used as a text in class. Though I would not name any of the three as a favorite now, I suspect their influence may still show. I was writing poetry fairly regularly during my college years, but I never consciously studied a poem to see "how it was done," nor read a book on prosody or a poet's discussion of the process. If such books existed during World War II, I was not aware of them, and of course there were no poetry readings.

When I outgrew this phase -- this need to write poems as some people write passionate letters they do not mail -- I stopped writing altogether. "Life" took over: marriage, jobs, graduate school, friends. Fortunately one of my jobs was in a library and I took books home, including volumes of poetry. I also took courses that dealt with

34

folktales, myths and traditional ballads at Indiana University.

In 1953 my mother died. Whenever someone asks me the inevitable question, "What made you become a poet?" I remember a calm, sunny afternoon a few weeks after her death, when I sat in a lovely backyard in Evanston, Illinois and felt an immense need to put some of what I felt about her death and that particular afternoon into a poem: to "say" my feelings, vent them, put them into some order, some context I could understand. If the impulse was therapeutic, it was also the start of my "real" writing. I was 29, and it was the first poem I had written in about 8 years. After that small, awkward poem, so hard to write, I knew I never wanted to stop making poems again.

During my college years, writing poems was an amateur activity, a natural means to channel feeling and imagination, as it is for many young people in love; the idea of "becoming a writer" never occurred to me. But now I began my training, which consisted of reading all the volumes of poetry and little magazines I could lay my hands on, teaching myself to read for instruction as well as pleasure, and setting myself exercises. There were no creative writing classes and few handbooks on craft then. My apprenticeship at this stage was a matter of hit-and-miss, lucky hunches and wild goose chases, a game of hide-and-seek with the masters I was looking for. It lacked the sensibly planned approach that a university program or a master/tutor might have provided; I wasted a lot of time. But it also provided the joys of accidental discovery: stumbling on books that changed my life and, now and then, writing a poem I felt sure no one had ever written before (although they had). I learned about traditional forms and metrics, since most of the poems published in those days employed metric or syllabic patterns and used rhyme and assonance. I worked in formal patterns for a while, but eventually returned to free verse because I found the echoes of the formal masters too strong for my incubating voice. When I wrote a sonnet, it got away from me, not only the language but the stance -- feeling, attitude -- became tenth-rate Keats.

My husband was and is my best critic. We were discovering the New Critics, whom we read together: Eliot's essays, Cleanth Brooks, Richards, Empson, Blackmur, Ransom. We read Pound's ABC of Reading and Auden's "Making, Knowing and Judging," which became part of The Dyer's Hand. I was getting an education. But I was getting another kind of education as well. Two daughters arrived four years apart. The question of whether a writer can live the traditional life of wife and mother without injury to her writing is of deep concern to many women poets and novelists. We have moving statements by Adrienne Rich, Tillie Olson and Ruth Whitman among others about the conflicts and deprivations they suffered. I can only speak for myself, and I was determined to have both. There is no question that bringing up small children without help takes, and takes away, a tremendous amount of time and energy. Not only that; the kind of energy -- the giving of one's spirit, mind and body to a child who needs that nourishment for growth as a plant needs carbohydrates for photosynthesis -- is similar to the energy that goes into making poems. But the process is reciprocal; watching one's child become a person is not only infinitely gratifying and humanizing, it is also instructive about growth, transformation, possibility: matters that poets deal with.

Two fortunate circumstances helped to keep me writing steadily during these years. One was a group of poet friends in the area which met at regular intervals; the other was my appointment as the poetry reviewer of a Chicago newspaper with a fair amount of interest in, and space for, current books of poetry. It was a free-lance job, manageable at home, and it meant that I was reading most of the poetry being published, and reading it carefully and critically. It required me to try and understand each poet's intention, to honor it, to evaluate the book's success partly in terms of this intention and to sum up my conclusions succinctly. If nothing else, the job forced me to think hard about poetry, and in retrospect I consider these years as a reviewer a tough but essential part of my apprenticeship.

Although I began to publish in the magazines during the mid-Fifties and continued to publish regularly, my first book of poems did not come out until 1965, when I was 41. I had written a great deal of poetry since that afternoon in 1953, but I threw most of it away. (I still consider the wastebasket one of my masters.)

Of course my apprenticeship did not end with the publication of a book. But for convenience I'll end my story here, as though it were an old-fashioned story and book publication the wedding. In reality, as we all know, apprenticeship, like life after the wedding, goes on indefinitely. In some ways it gets harder. Once the tools, tricks and secrets of the trade become second nature, you lose the attention to technique which has served as a margin of safety. Suddenly you are nakedly exposed to the dangerous process of bringing a poem into existence. You become less sure; you understand why writers put off writing, know the fear of failure, which has nothing to do with what the world calls failure. You are asked to dive into the pool, and you did not know the deep end was that deep. The models in the back of your head have fallen silent, and the rules want to be broken. If anything, the process of making a poem becomes more mysterious and terrifying.

How did I become a writer? All writers must ask themselves that question. And what if things had been different? What if I had not come to English as a second language, a circumstance that gave me a special awareness of its riches and inventiveness, its unlimited possibilities of nuance? What if I had had the opportunity for study in a formal creative writing program instead of learning to play by ear? What if my mother had not died when she did; if I had not had children; if I had not studied myths and folktales and so found the treasure mountain of metaphor which I plunder for my poems? Who can tell what might have been or what has been lost? I have only hindsight, which tells me that everything in my life has been grist for the writer's mill. Last year I wrote a small poem called "Fenestration," which plays on the architectural vs. the surgical meaning of that word. For the existence of that poem I give thanks to a job I had 25 years earlier as a receptionist in an otolaryngologist's office. It's enough to make me believe nothing is ever wasted, that there is only gain, accrual, seed lying in wait.

RETURN

a memoir

It is September 1983, and I am in Germany, a tourist in what should have been my own country. My husband and I are visiting Hamburg, the city I left, with my mother and sister, 44 years ago. My father, a teacher, had become a political refugee after Hitler came to power in 1933 and had been living outside of Germany most of the time since then. In June of 1939, three months before the outbreak of World War II, we followed him to the United States. This is my first trip back.

I am the only one in my family who has postponed the return all these years, and even now the need for the journey feels more like an obligation than a wish. My mother died in the United States in 1953, and my lonely father, who after her death became a restless transcontinental traveler, has been dead seven years now. He had been the remaining link to my childhood, and his trips back and forth had given me the connection between here and there and at the same time spared me the pain, the conflicting feelings I thought I would have to confront if I myself went back. Now the connection is broken, and it is up to me to restore it. I've decided I must come face to face with my childhood which, for reasons of history, was difficult, but which was cushioned by the love of not just my parents, but also three grandparents.

All these years I have lived with memories of that love, and they have become painful because they are suffused with the adult knowledge of decent lives ruled by an increasingly barbarous history which eventually destroyed them. They have been as painful as the out-and-out bad memories of the terror we lived under in the Third Reich, where you could disappear for not giving the Hitler salute, for a disparaging remark about the government, for listening to a foreign radio station or even owning a short-wave radio because that meant you might be listening. I remember the morning my mother and grandmother set out to search for my father, who had not come home from an appointment the night before, and found he had been arrested by the Gestapo. By pure chance he was released a few frightening days later; one of the lucky ones.

I've often looked at a picture of my father, taken in 1933, just before he had to leave us -- how young and thin and sad he looked. I've made the connection between my spirited mother's death at 54 and the hardships of supporting my sister and me, alone, with too little money, with no sense of the future and a constant sense of danger. I've inherited a book of facsimiles of medieval manuscripts my father inscribed to my mother with a small 13th-century lyric that told her she would always be locked in his heart because the key was lost. Below the poem was written, "In a hard time." It is dated Christmas 1933.

I have lived with such memories and mementos and I was afraid others would come at me if I went back to the old places, more than I could handle. Surely the streets and buildings would release things I had forgotten. For a long time I did not want to take that chance.

But now I am in Hamburg, and I am not alone. My American-born husband is with me, a hedge against nostalgia, a constant reminder that I am temporary here and my life is elsewhere. We have been married since we were nineteen, and he was close to my parents. He knows the old stories and has seen the photographs. But he is free of memories.

*

I don't know if I was more afraid that, after the bombings, Hamburg would be unrecognizable to me, or that it would look exactly as it had and so insist on the poignancy of memory. As it turns out, the question is moot. During our four days here I can't predict what will and will not touch me. Nor, in retrospect, can I account for my reactions. For years, I did not want to be German, wanted nothing to do with German traditions. More recently, I have come to love the language again, through reading and translating it and going to see German films. Still, I had not imagined that it would be such a pleasure to hear German spoken all around me again. In spite of my rustiness this total immersion is pure joy. I eavesdrop on people in restaurants, in the theater, on the street, curious not just about what they are saying, but how they say it. Paradoxically, German has taken on for me the magic of a second language; ever so slightly distanced, it teases with a faintly exotic glamour.

Then there is the Alster, the river that runs through the city and forms a lake in the center. The skyline is defined by it, just as the skyline at home in Chicago is defined by Lake Michigan. And just as Chicagoans who live miles from the Lake are proud and proprietary when they show it to visitors, I am proud and proprietary when I present the Alster to my husband. On the day we look up my old apartment in one of Hamburg's less attractive neighborhoods, we decide to go there by boat, rather than subway. The small white boats, still called steamers from the days before diesel fuel, run every half hour, crisscrossing the Alster and then entering one of its many canals. We move beneath overhanging willows and the round arches of thick stone bridges. From the backs of houses, gardens slope down to the water; it has been a long, warm summer and the roses are still in bloom. I am strangely affected by these sights, though views of the Alster were the exception, not the rule, for me as a child, and I don't know if my response comes from personal memory, or if such images - water, white boats, stone bridges, arching willows - are universal images of lost childhood.

The gulls, survivors from way back, are still at their scavenging trade on the water. And I suddenly remember the hawk that came year after year to roost on the steeple of a church near the riverbank, when I was little. It was a sort of emblem and its annual arrival seemed important, or perhaps it was only made so by my mother, who used to play that she was the hawk trying to gobble me up when I snuggled against her. She made up a song about it, accompanying herself on the piano with several strong chords. The song was something like a tiny prelude to a non-existent fugue, and it was in a minor key, but it did not seem sad to me.

*

I am moved by the Alster, but when I stand in front of the red brick apartment building I lived in for six years, I feel only strangeness. We moved here after my father lost his job and we could no longer afford to live in our large, ground-floor apartment in another part of town. I take a couple of pictures with my Minolta automatic, but there is no click inside me. Though I am sure I have the right building, it doesn't quite look as I have remembered it. The proportions are different and I don't remember the plantings in front. Nor were there any cars, parked German-narrow-street style, half-on, half-off the sidewalk,

40

when we lived here. No one on this street had a car then, and it was fine for hopscotch and roller-skating. But I suspect I would not have been any more deeply affected if the street and the building had remained exactly as they were. I look up at the second-floor windows and try to resurrect the child I was, to will her image into being, watch her move through the four small rooms, past the black grand piano with its fringed, silk-embroidered shawl, make her look at me so I can meet my long-ago self, feel the loss of a life. But it does not work. The real red brick building I have remembered for 44 years becomes surreal when I face it; it blocks the imagination. The child is a puppet. I feel nothing for her. The real child lives inside me, and though I do not understand why, she is more alive in her house of memory away from here. Nor does my presence on this street bring forth anything I did not already know about the 9-year-old, the older daughter, carrying the burden of necessary secrecy about her father, whom she thought of as a hero and wanted to speak about publicly and proudly. I force myself to think of her, and of the 14-year-old who, on the most beautiful, flower-laden day in April, was seized by an extremity of sadness and found herself shocked and bewildered by that inappropriate response to beauty. I conjure up the adolescent who rehearsed in front of the mirror, dressing up, changing her accent. Of course she wanted to be an actress and throw herself off a cliff for the sake of love, at least on stage, as she had seen a famous actress do in a play about Sappho. I think of the nights she was unable to sleep because she was too much in love with her literature teacher, an intense, learned woman who, I now know, looked unattractive and sexless. The actress and the teacher were what we would call role models now, but the child knew only that she was in love. Passion was still asexual, and the first instance of falling in love with a young man a year off. I think of the day she wrote and passed a note to a classmate, and it was intercepted by a teacher who was an enthusiastic party member. The note contained a joke about a top government official. I remember her terror, the fear of the knock on the door that would take her mother away forever, and the gratitude -- beyond any gratitude felt since -- when the teacher did not turn her in.

When we visit some of my childhood haunts, I discover odd lapses of memory. For instance, in the municipal park -- a huge area with beautiful gardens, lagoons, woods and restaurants -- I instantly recognize the green field used for ballplaying and kite flying, but it takes me a long time to remember that the golden-domed planetarium at one end of it had always been there. Though I must have walked past it dozens, perhaps hundreds, of times, its image had dropped away like a lost photograph. And when we trace my old route between home and school, I cannot always connect the images I remember with the ones I see. We walk on the bridge over the canal the child crossed every day, deep in thought, in an argument with herself, so strongly impelled to articulate some declaration in her mind, to make it real, that she would turn her head toward the water and move her lips, perhaps even mumble, hoping no one noticed. Yet when we walk over what must be the same bridge, I do not recognize it except by its location. It sends no signals, stirs up no emotions. I am astonished to discover that memory is a cloister, that the life inside cuts itself off from the world than set it going.

On the other hand I am stunned to find, two blocks from our old apartment, the tiny branch of my mother's Savings and Loan Association still there, though it has a new face. And a few doors down there is still the small bookstore whose rental library was my grandmother's source of mysteries, English detective novels in translation mostly. I am wondering if the owner could possibly be the same, but I remind myself how unlikely that is. After all, anyone middle-aged in 1939 would be dead by now. I have a hard time convincing myself of the passage of time in this city, being used to a country where change is a way of life, where the town's A&P is closed overnight and the famous old restaurant worthy of a 50-mile drive is suddenly a boat and garden shop. Here I am the protagonist of a Rip Van Winkle story, except it is reversed; time has stood still, there has been no war. Only I have changed.

*

From my old street we walk to my grandmother's old apartment, a 10-minute walk. I am elated to remember the way; a small triumph, proof of some deep connection after all. But the bulldog Ego, whom I used to meet on one of the two streets we take, is no longer there, and I recognize none of the buildings. I doubt that it is because they are all postwar buildings; many of them look as if they must have watched me pass through this street countless times. What I recognize without surprise, because it looks exactly as it does in my memory, is the round red brick archway leading into the apartment complex for retired persons where my grandmother lived.

It still reminds me of the Grimm Brothers' tale of the goose girl, and I half expect a faithful horse's head to look down at me -- Fallada, whom the abused princess can trust with her woeful secret. But there is no Fallada, and my grandmother is not at the first floor window behind the begonias, waiting for us to arrive for a Sunday dinner of rumpsteak fixed with butter and onions and accompanied by white asparagus, delicacies my mother could not afford. I imagine her four years after we left, in another June, picking up her purse and a blanket and running from that burning building, never to return. Fifty-five thousand people died in that fire-bombing, but she survived to live through the postwar years without food or heat, without the familiar objects of her past, though the past was all she had left. Widowed young, she had lost her first son in the First World War; her second son, my father, was in the United States, and we, her daughter-in-law and her two grandchildren, had followed him. She was completely alone.

Now, miraculously, the building looks exactly as it did when she lived there. The restoration, like the restoration everywhere in this phoenix of a country, has been meticulous. Too meticulous, I think. There should be some reminder that for years these buildings lay in ruins, that my grandmother is dead, that I have come back to a different time, a different place. More than half of the city's residential area was destroyed in the summer of 1943. Where does it come from, the strength, the faith, that lets people put stone on stone again, not grudgingly or hastily, but carefully, lovingly, as though this time the city would last forever?

*

There is one more pilgrimage to be made in Hamburg, to the house whose top floor was the apartment of my other grandparents, my mother's parents. We buy a map, take the elevated train, and find the house. We have been told it was the only one on the block left standing after the 1943 bombings. Ironically, my grandparents, who could have survived the war in their own home, had gone east to be with their youngest daughter in a small town on the Baltic Sea and were later caught in a long, terrible flight from the advancing Russian army.

I recognize the house and am not bothered by the new buildings surrounding it, since I have no memory of what the Wagnerstrasse looked like in the days when we got off at this same train station and walked the half block to the house. I have remembered the house in isolation, surrounded by empty space, as if the bombing had already taken place. Again I feel compelled to stand across the street and take a picture, as if memory would be sure to let me down or my American daughters would some day need a snapshot of the windows behind which their unknown great-grandparents had lived. Behind those windows stood the cactus which was cut down many times and always insisted on growing up to the ceiling again. During the Christmas season it was backed by a fir tree hung with china angels, silvery trumpets and delicious edible ornaments: nonpareils and chocolate wreaths filled with orange liqueur. But there is no cactus in the window now, and the music-box, whose brass cylinder entertained us with selections from Verdi and Offenbach, which would be set for either orchestral or harp arrangement, is gone. I have no curiosity about who lives there now. I know the inside, those rooms, although, my cousin later tells me, I have rearranged them. I have set them down in a poem, "My Grandmother's Gold Pin," written 16 years ago: rooms with magic objects, my grandfather and grandmother moving among them, and I don't know if what I remember are the rooms of childhood or the rooms of the poem, but it does not matter.

What matters is that there are memories, images that bring back my grandparents, that I have been able to rescue them from their second death, the real one, which is being forgotten. What matters also is that these images tell the truth about the rich pleasures and the easy, generous kind of love that can be the special province of grandparents. Mine were middle-class children of the 19th-century,

44

brought up to be civilized in mind and heart, to be gentle as well as genteel. We would call them innocent now. It was a time when human perfectibility seemed possible and the barbarism of the modern totalitarian state was unimaginable. Such devastating knowledge should have been spared them, I thought when I wrote the poem, and standing in front of their house, I think it again.

AFTERWORD

As I finish writing this, six weeks later, the small wound over my shinbone -- the result of a fall on a subway platform in Hamburg -- is only a slight bruise, already yellow, adapting to my skin. It's the only mark, the only visible change I have brought back and soon it too will be gone. Then there will be only this new cluster of impressions, which are just beginning to sink, feel for their niche, their share of meaning. But they will remain a separate layer; they have nothing to do with the images I have carried with me for 44 years. I know now that my childhood is an inviolate country. It has sealed its borders against me, its creator, and is impervious to any attempt at breaking and entering. Its characters and settings are immutably fixed in the second language of memory. I have come and gone, but I have not disturbed them. Their positions are held; their sadness and happiness will not change.

TWO STRAINS:
SOME THOUGHTS ABOUT ENGLISH WORDS

For someone like myself, who writes in a language she was not born into, the second language assumes and retains a special fascination. We absorb our first language long before we speak it, and we learn to speak it fluently without ever becoming conscious of the learning process. The second language -- in my case English, learned during adolescence -- is different, and the consciousness of the difference is enhanced by a European school background which stresses grammar, spelling and etymology. It's true that after some time in a new country the process of learning the language also becomes unconscious: you are suddenly aware that you are no longer translating, but are thinking and even dreaming in the adopted language. And for many of us it is the native language that recedes and becomes the "second language." Nevertheless, the exoticism of a language learned at a distance remains for the non-native; it hovers in the back of one's mind, to surface on certain occasions.

Translating invariably provides such occasions. It's impossible to translate anything from one language into another without thinking of the natures, and/or structures, of these languages, the differences in their traditions, for example, and in their syntactic approach to expressiveness. The translator of poetry is forced to think hardest of all. The considerations in this essay ultimately proceed from such hard thinking about a poem by Marie Luise Kaschnitz, which I was translating from German into English. The problem started with the title, "Die Länder, die Meere," which could be rendered equally correctly as either "The Countries, the Oceans," or "The Lands, the Seas." The choice is beyond accuracy; it comes down to sound, as well as very fine differences -- vibrations, almost -- of connotation. "The Countries, the Oceans" reproduces the syllabic and stress patterns of the German; on the other hand, "The Lands, the Seas," gives us words that are Germanic in origin. The similarity of L<u>änder</u> and <u>lands</u> as to sound is tempting. The words <u>countries</u> and <u>oceans</u> have connotations of geographic entity, while <u>lands</u> and <u>seas</u> have an additional generic sense of earth and water. As translator, I had to decide which of these connotations was closer to the poet's intention.

In the body of the same poem, I had to deal with the phrase, "schlafende Griechin," which refers to the remains of an antique female statue on the coast of Sicily, but refers also to the poet herself, since the poem deals with the fluidity of past and present in the memory of old age. My first translation of the phrase as "sleeping Greek statue," though technically correct, bothered me. I knew sleeping was not quite the word I wanted, but I couldn't find the right one, the one I knew was hiding somewhere. Days later someone in my family made some mention of dormant plants, and my word jumped out at me. Dormant, from French dormir, means sleeping, of course, but tradition has endowed the word (ever since La Belle au Bois dormante?) with a future, the implied certainty of an awakening. Though our experience tells us that sleeping creatures will most likely wake up, the word sleeping, unlike dormant, offers no such certainty. In the context of the Kaschnitz poem, the built-in expectation, with its suggestion of a doze rather than a deep sleep, was just what I wanted, and I marveled again at the richness of the language which allowed me such delicious choices.

It's a commonplace, of course, that English is the richest European language, and that it got that way because of a series of invaders into the British Isles, who left successive layers of language. English words remind us of the presence of Celts, Scots, Romans and Danes, but their two dominant strains derive from the 5th century invasions of the Angles and Saxons, two Germanic tribes, and the conquest by the French-speaking Normans in the 11th century. The amalgam makes English both less "pure" and more abundant than other languages; compare the sizes of dictionaries.

In many areas we have virtually a dual language, with words from both strains interchangeable as to meaning, though not necessarily "feeling" or "flavor." Because of custom and convenience, I will refer to the two strains as "Germanic" (i.e. Anglo-Saxon and Scandinavian) and "Latinate" respectively, even though "Latinate," while accommodating all the Romance languages, technically leaves out English words deriving from Greek roots, of which there are many, especially in science and philosophy. (It's also true that some Germanic words ultimately go back to the Latin.)

There is no real difference in meaning between <u>amiable</u> and <u>friendly,</u> <u>forbid</u> and <u>prohibit,</u> <u>respond</u> and <u>answer,</u> <u>purchase</u> and <u>buy,</u> <u>gift</u> and <u>present,</u> <u>vivacious</u> and <u>lively,</u> but the feeling of the Latinate words is somewhat more formal, more "educated." Sometimes the difference in feeling is greater. A <u>forest</u> is more impressive than the <u>woods,</u> <u>climate</u> is more inclusive than <u>weather,</u> a <u>chamber</u> is more elegant than a <u>room,</u> a <u>mansion</u> is a very large <u>house,</u> an <u>object</u> is slightly more exalted than a <u>thing,</u> a <u>breeze</u> is a gentle sort of <u>wind.</u> A <u>corpuscular,</u> <u>mendacious</u> <u>monarch</u> is a puffed-up <u>fat</u> <u>liar</u> of a <u>king.</u> <u>Foliage,</u> a collective noun, encompasses a mass of leaves and so is more inclusive than the simple plural <u>leaves,</u> but it keeps us from experiencing the visual and tactile image of each individual leaf.

<u>Sex</u> is Latinate, but the so-called four-letter words for specific sexual parts and acts are Anglo-Saxon nouns and verbs. Writers (and non-writers) know the difficulty of finding an appropriate "language of love" in English, since the Germanic words still offend many people and the Latinate ones feel "clinical." Euphemisms are all we have to fill the gap. We all remember D.H. Lawrence's attempt, in <u>Lady</u> <u>Chatterley's</u> <u>Lover,</u> to "purify" the taboo sexual words by using them in a work of literature. It's not surprising that he failed. A writer may have a great, and nearly instantaneous, influence on the literary style of his period, but he cannot single-handedly change deeply embedded attitudes toward words, especially when they carry with them age-old associations of fear and shame. Preference for Latinate over Germanic words connected with bodily functions applies even where the Germanic words are permissible. <u>Fragrance,</u> <u>perfume</u> and <u>odor</u> are "nicer" than <u>smell,</u> and it's more genteel to <u>perspire</u> than to <u>sweat.</u>

We don't have synonyms for everything, of course. The Norman and Plantagenet kings and their aristocracy superimposed on the Anglo-Saxon society a culture different in kind and broader in scope, a culture which moreover acted as a natural conduit for literature, architecture, science, philosophy and music from the European continent. While Latin remained the language of the law and the Church, French was the language of the ruling class and the school until the 14th century, when the fusion we call English became the official language. No wonder then that English has few Germanic words that refer to the intellectual life, virtually none for concepts in the sciences, and in the case of the arts, only for their simplest forms and aspects. Even in the areas of cooking, dress, furniture and manners, the language relies heavily on French-derived words. On the other hand, the plain, short Anglo-Saxon words for the necessities of an agricultural life, for basic relationships, for our bodies and their organic processes, and for the natural world, have stuck: birth, death, growth, sickness; earth, water, sun, moon; mother, father, child, love; hammer, nail, wrench; wall, door, window; hand, foot, bone, blood, breath, hair, tooth; sheep, cow; tree, wheat. Except for the technical terms of science, we have no Latinate equivalents for most of these nouns, though we do have Latinate adjectives that refer to them: native, mortal, terrestrial, aquatic, lunar, solar, corporeal, dexterous, pedestrian, bovine, arboreal, etc.

Languages change. When we consider the enormous changes that occurred between the writing of Beowulf and Chaucer, and again in the two centuries between Chaucer and Shakespeare, it is astonishing that, four centuries later, we understand Shakespeare as well as we do. English, a Germanic language, is heavily stressed and employs a Germanic mode of syntax. Nevertheless, despite its Germanic roots and patterns, English has shifted its vocabulary heavily in the direction of Latinate words during the past two centuries. This shift has been accelerating in our own time. The inroads of general education, of science, technology and the social sciences all favor such a shift. Certainly the language of Shakespeare and the author of the King James version of the Bible (who did not use words like solar, aquatic and pedestrian) was much more clearly Germanic in its vocabulary, as well as in the use of certain constructions. One thinks of the many Germanic words that must have disappeared from usage, in addition to those we still know; words like dale, now taken over by valley, and reckon, which has become figure. One thinks of the flower which once was a bloom, and of the deaf-and-dumb who have become deafmutes, because of the more recent equation of dumb with stupid. And surely English must have had Germanic nouns for such basic concepts as "innocence" and "jealousy" and "mystery" at one time.*

One has only to listen to talk shows and interviews on radio and television to be made aware of the influx of Latinate words in everyday speech. But I am ultimately concerned with the words that poets use, and how they use them. I think it's safe to say that Pound's insistence on the plainest word (that modernist with the purist heart!) is not their foremost aesthetic concern. It seems that poetic diction is changing, but at a much slower rate than general speech. Poets are conservators of language. They have no use for jargon, which much of our current speech consists of, and they like words that have been invested with history and weighted with feeling; words that have overtones, reverberations; words that set off a chain reaction of associations. And they have traditionally dealt with birth, death, love, the natural world and the humbler aspects of human existence. But the natural world is becoming less and less available as a subject, and that fact coupled with the move away from metered verse may additionally change poetic diction. It's too soon to tell.

Germanic nouns and verbs (except in the -ing formations) are words of one or two syllables. We think of them as strong, simple, immediate, visceral. They touch our elemental nature. We connect Latinate words with exoticism, sonority, decorum, wit and education; with the expression of ideas, and a high degree of conceptualization. The suffixes we use to extend words in order to express quality, process and states of being are Latinate: moderation, radiation, bondage, sexuality, happiness. Word(s) is Germanic, but vocabulary is Latinate, and wordiness a mix of a Germanic root word with a Latinate suffix. Such suffixes add to the number of syllables, of course, and we do indeed tend to equate "Latinate" with "polysyllabic," ignoring the huge number of short, specific words which have acquired the same status of common household words that we connect with Germanic ones. It's true, though, that words of more than two syllables in English are almost exception Latinate. Most four-syllable words and English are almost without exception Latinate. Most four-syllable words and some three-syllable ones, receive two stresses, usually a primary and a secondary one: estuary, memorandum, eternity, recognize. Obviously, sound, including weight, is as much a factor as sense in word selection. A poet who wants to cluster stresses, who hammers away as

----

*It seems ironic that the word tradition is Latinate. But of course the very awareness of tradition, and hence the coinage of such a word, implies a self-conscious, sophisticated society.

Hopkins did, has to rely on a heavily Germanic diction, while a writer of light verse or social satire may choose a long, lightly accented line.* When Richard Wilbur has Pangloss tell us about the joys of venereal disease, which is after all a gift from Venus, and when he translates Molière's sophisticated comedies of manners, the cultivated artifice of the society is made abundantly clear in the tripping meter and the witty feminine rhymes. Such lines as

Since women are (from natural reticence)
Reluctant to declare their sentiments,
And since the honor of our sex requires,
That we conceal our amorous desires

leave no doubt as to the spirit in which they are to be taken. And when Edward Dorn begins his poem "Song" with the lines

Again, I am made the occurrence
Of one of her charms. Let me
Explain. An occupier
Of one of the waves of her intensity

he sets the tone, telling us to expect a love poem which is elegant and keeps its distance.

In The Truth of Poetry, Michael Hamburger mentions Yves Bonnefoy's discussion of French, as compared to English, poetry. The tradition of French poetry, Bonnefoy says, is abstract; it deals with essences. French poets want generic words, unlike English poets, who want the specific. He thinks the difference arises from the languages themselves. As a result, those French poets whom English-speaking ones have particularly admired for their concrete imagery, rank low in the esteem of their countrymen. Surely Bonnefoy's discoveries show some parallels to our feeling about Latinate and Germanic words and underscore the Germanic tradition of poetry in English.

----

*All histories of versification in English tell us of the overwhelming preference for the disyllabic, especially iambic, foot over the anapest and dactyl.

I have been looking at some well-worn anthology pieces by 20th-century poets, curious to see what I would discover about their vocabulary. English being by definition a fusion of languages, it would of course be impossible to write a purely Latinate poem, at least one that used syntax, since conjunction, articles, numbers and auxiliary verbs are Germanic. It would be much easier to write one in an exclusively Germanic vocabulary, but it wouldn't be likely to come about unless the poet consciously worked at it. In "Richard Cory," the first poem I looked at, Robinson reserves all the "fancy" words for Cory. The common people, of whom the speaker is one, they who "went without the meat and cursed the bread," are uniformly endowed with short, chiefly Germanic, words, and the Latinate ones, like "bullet," "pavement," "place" and "human," are of the sort that by now feel quite common. But Richard Cory, the rich man of the town, is "imperially slim," "clean favored," "quietly arrayed" and "admirably schooled in every grace." The shoe fits.

Dylan Thomas, that lover of strong, old words, whose "tumbledown tongue" retrieved so many of them from obscurity, does something similar in his poem "In My Craft Or Sullen Art." Richard Cory is a man set apart by money and position and, it turns out, by some grief or terror so great it drives him to suicide. Thomas' poet-speaker, who "labour(s) by singing light" to praise the quotidian lovers, who "lie abed/with all their griefs in their arms" and are unaware of his existence, is also a man set apart. Thomas' diction throughout consists of short, simple words (including the Latinate, but common, rhyme words "rages," "stages," "wages," "pages" and "ages"), except when he refers to the possibility of fame,

Not for ambition or bread
Or the strut and trade of charms,
On the ivory stages,

and to his work, which is "exercised in the still night." "Refusal to Mourn the Death, by Fire, of a Child in London," that magnificent poem, whose first thirteen lines are one driving, onrushing sentence made up of one and two-syllable words of primarily Germanic origin (emphasized by the heavy alliteration), stuns the reader with its exceptions. Besides the religious words, there is the line "The majesty and burning of the child's death," followed by the statement that the poet refuses to demean this majesty "With any further/Elegy of innocence and youth." Anyone who has looked at Thomas' notebooks has seen the long lists of alternative words he used to write in the margins, and so knows the extreme care with which he choose his vocabulary. For this reader, "majesty" seems inevitable, the only word large, solemn and authoritative enough to do what Thomas wants it to do here. It is something of a public word, carrying overtones of great and stately ceremony. On the other hand, "Elegy" and "innocence" become pejorative in this context, take on an air of sentimentality and artifice that would trivialize the child's death. The poet's statement of refusal is followed immediately by the wonderful, simple line, "Deep with the first dead lies London's daughter," a line whose sound and sense tells us everything about the poet's feeling toward this death.

Wallace Stevens is often cited as a poet with a heavily Latinate diction. One thinks of such titles as "The Auroras of Autumn," "Memoirs of a Magnifico" and "The Revolutionists Stop for Orangeade." One thinks of the exuberantly witty use of words in "The Comedian as the Letter C," of the luxurious exoticism of "Sea Surface Full of Clouds," and the flavor of romantic alienation in "Esthetique du Mal," with lines like

The tongue caresses these exacerbations,
They press it as epicure, distinguishing
Themselves from its essential savor,
Like hunger that feeds on its own hungriness

But the fact is that Stevens' vocabulary is chosen for the occasion of each poem. "A High-Toned Old Christian Woman" is a splendid example of how he plays off Latinate against Germanic words. The poem is a kind of mock-battle, a joyous, frisky contest between sound effects. "Sunday Morning" and "Peter Quince at the Clavier," poems which are at once philosophical and sensuous, consists of that inimitable blend of flavors and textures which makes Stevens' language so truly marvelous. But there are many short poems whose language is quite plain. In Harmonium, for example, a large number of them come close to the Imagist ideal, as far as diction is concerned. The famous Tennesseean jar, for one. (Sometimes the titles are foolers. The only thing "foreign" about "Memoirs of a Magnifico" is its title.) Throughout Stevens' work, and especially in the posthumous poems with their revealing and disarming simplicity, we find poems of predominantly Germanic diction. I think that it's the placement, rather than frequency, of exotic words, as well as their flamboyance, that shocks the reader into regarding Stevens' vocabulary as more Latinate than it actually is; for example, the piling-up and juxtaposition of "caliper," "divine ingenue," "companion," and "fragrance of vegetal" in the first stanza of "Let's Look at the Lilacs," and the sudden extravagance of words like "inflections," "innuendoes," "barbaric glass" and "bawds of euphony" in the otherwise spare and chaste "Thirteen Ways of Looking at a Blackbird."

Theodore Roethke's diction is heavily Germanic, as befits a poet who wrote about the humblest forms of organic life and the naked life of feeling. In "Elegy for Jane," this applies not only to the verbs and nouns, but to the adjectives -- and Roethke's poems are filled with adjectives. Such adjectives as "pickerel," "spiny," "maimed" and "bleached" (in conjunction with "valleys") are hard to find elsewhere in modern poetry. Significantly, the only line in which the verb-noun combination is Latinate, is "And she balanced in the delight of her thought." The other Roethke poem known to every undergraduate is, of course, "My Papa's Waltz." Looking at that poem freshly, from my new perspective, turned into a happy surprise for me. Not only does the poem, with its triple-stressed lines, beat time in our heads, as Roethke's father did on that of his son, but its language instructs us abundantly about the nature of the activity and the attitudes of the participants. There is not a word of more than two syllables in the poem, except one, countenance; and look what it accomplishes:

The whiskey on your breath
Could make a small boy dizzy;
But I hung on like death:
Such waltzing was not easy.

We romped until the pans
Slid from the kitchen shelf;
My mother's countenance
Could not unfrown itself

Roethke needed no more than a single word to tell us how the mother felt about such goings-on.

A few old favorites, chosen at random, out of curiosity, with no intention of proving anything. But something has been proven for me after all: the persistence of how we feel towards words, the endurance of our sense of their associations, their surfaces, their taste -- in short, our sense of their rightness for our purposes.

We can't always be sure whether we are responding to sense or sound. We think of earth and breath, for example, as strong, affecting words. But is that because of what they mean - because we connect them with our mothers and fathers, with our own organic life, our most basic needs - or is it because our earliest excursions into language, or perhaps some factors in our nervous system, determine our feeling about short, explosive words? In How Does a Poem Mean, John Ciardi presents a paraphrase of Williams' "A Sort of Song." What he calls paraphrase is virtually a translation of Williams' simple words, precise in meaning and frictive in sound, into blurrier, more general and more archaically "poetic" ones. The object of Ciardi's deliberately "bad" poem is, of course, to emphasize the importance of word choice in the overall effect of a poem, since its denotative meaning, the "message," is not altered. Beyond this intention, the paraphrase makes evident once again the wealth of the English vocabulary, as well as the receding of some once common words into archaisms. Williams' "wait," "split" and "rocks" become Ciardi's "bide," "cleave" and "crags." All six are Germanic, but only Williams' are in common usage now. Ciardi substitutes "spiritual and material" for Williams' "the poeple and the stones," a substitution of philosophical, non-specific, polysyllabic adjectives for Williams' nouns. The effect is one of greater remove from the experience of the poem, a toning-down of its urgency. Ciardi's point came at me backwards, when I read the two versions to a group of old people, all of whom preferred Ciardi's. Brought up on bad inspirational verse, they wanted the distance; they felt uncomfortable with poems whose words bore down on them. One woman commended Ciardi especially for changing Williams' "snake" to "serpent." Snakes gave her the shivers, she said, but serpents did not threaten her. Though the literary lesson backfired, I can think of no better proof of Ciardi's contention and, for that matter, of the power of the word in our lives -- in this instance, a magic power restoring the ancient identity of the thing and its name.

"AFTER WHISTLER": A POEM IN SEARCH OF ITSELF

Note: I rarely keep drafts for finished poems. This one was different. It was an experiment, a way of inducing, or conjuring, a poem from scratch -- a new experience for me, and I was curious about it. It took four weeks to get from start to finish, and two months after I had completed the final version, I read over the twenty drafts and tried to figure out how I had gotten from there to here. That is to say, this essay is an exercise in memory and rationalization, an example of hindsight, and therefore a much more orderly and controlled process than writing a poem. For that reason it is also less than trustworthy. Still I assume that the author knows as much about his or her poem as anyone else, and with luck a little more. What was revealed to me is something I had always believed but never seen so plainly demonstrated: that the poem's formal demands are infinitely adaptable to one's changing drafts, but that they insist on being satisfied.

The poem began as an attempt to break a long-lasting dry spell, or "writer's block." Generally I've learned to be patient and wait for language to give in eventually and throw me a bone to start on. This bone is usually a scrap of language, a phrase or succession of phrases, in which the rhythm and syntax are already determined and seem unalterable, and therefore make certain formal demands regarding the language that must follow. In other words, the beginning of a pattern is set up, so that the existing language can generate more, and similar, language and move the poem forward. This isn't to say that the initial rush of language may not lead me astray, cause me to take a wrong turn, get into a blind alley, or simply peter out. But it does mean that there are clues for where the poem wants to go in its search for itself, its body, its ideal form.

On this occasion I hadn't been thrown a bone for six months, and I was desperate. I decided to will a poem into being. I found out that the search for the poem, never easy, was immensely difficult in this case because I lacked the pressure -- whatever that pressure may be -- which compulsively and authoritatively shapes the initial language fragment.

*

It was a bright, hot summer day and I was sitting in my yard. I decided to do something I had never done before: let my mind go blank and seize on the first image to swim into it. What came was a sense of whiteness, embodied in a vision of Emily Dickinson in her white dress and accompanied by the words "Going in White," which was the working title of the poem for a number of drafts. These two elements were almost instantly followed by the idea of the moon as an albino rose, and this in turn begot its contrary, the sun, composed of "mustard and urine." At one point during this succession of visual and verbal images, which came fast, much faster than it takes to tell about them, I saw out of the corner of my mind's eye a white cotton dress with an orange macrame belt. It was a dress I was wearing that summer, and I belted it with that orange belt because without something bright the dress was too boring, like a uniform. At this point in my mental chain of events I perceived the orange belt as a mitigation of pure, stark white, which had already taken on an ambiguous cast: as something absolute and perfect, a pure beauty, and because of that, opposed to life, which is after all impure. I could imagine a girl or young woman longing for such undefiled beauty, which is also the beauty of death and therefore dangerous to those who are susceptible to its attraction. (This wasn't thought out as logically as it sounds here, but I remember feeling a tug of ambiguity about the images, which is not unusual for me since my poems often seem to reflect a need to reconcile, or at least come to terms with, opposites. After my unconscious mind had given me the word pairings "albino rose" and "precious aberration" which are of course paradoxical, I couldn't help but sense, however dimly, my ambiguous feelings, though not until after the peculiar dialectic of what I assume to be common human thought) suggested the image of the lifegiving sun as being composed of such indelicate substances as mustard and urine.

By now I was thinking more consciously, though I still wasn't writing anything down but letting the images accumulate in my head. I decided to address a "you," the young girl or woman I was sensing -- "imagining" would be too strong a word -- as the protagonist of all that whiteness, to expand the "white" images and bring in the orange belt as a counterforce, like the sun. When I realized, a little later, that life preservers are orange I congratulated myself on my good luck of having glimpsed that belt; it seemed the perfect object of rescue.

Here then was my first draft:

1.
GOING IN WHITE

The moon rises
like Emily Dickinson.
An albino rose, you say,
precious in its aberration
for us tough ones, red and pink,
who are not hurt by the sun's
mustard and urine. You long for the pure
world without the double distortion
of light filtered through the air. You decide
to go in white. But when you stand,
a speechless bride, in the blanched
underworld of ice
and alabaster, the orange belt
you also chose will protect you
from staying too long.

I liked the idea of the frozen underworld, which I imagined as a cave
with stalactites and stalagmites, and I thought the "speechless bride"
was an image not only of white virginity, but of immobility as well. But
that part of the poem seemed too brief for the middle section it
obviously wanted to be. It needed expanding for the sake of the
poem's pace and balance:

2.
The moon rises
like Emily Dickinson.
An albino rose, you say,
precious in its aberration
for us tough ones, pink and red,
who are unharmed by the sun's
mustard and urine. You long for the pure
world without the double distortion
of light filtered through air.

You have decided to go in white.
But when you stand, a speechless bride,
in the blanched underworld
of alabaster and ice
and the pale moths,
blue-eyed like you,
fearlessly light on the back of your hand,
the orange belt, which you also chose,
will keep you from staying too long.

The pale moths as emissaries of death, or if not literal death, at least from a world of withdrawal, seemed all right to me, and at that point I left the middle section alone and turned my attention to the ending, which was too abrupt to be convincing. I realized it was the sudden turnabout, a kind of hairbreadth escape, which made it difficult to convert into a convincing conclusion. I thought that separating the ending syntactically, and putting a period and stanza break between it and the moth image, might create a sense of some distance and so make the reversal more credible:

3.
(First 9 lines same as above)
You have decided to wear white
so when you stand, a tearless bride,
in the underground fluorescence
of alabaster and ice
the pale moths, blue-eyed like you,
will light on the back of your hand.

But you've chosen an orange belt,
your narrow lifeline.

Well, that didn't do it: the ending still seemed like something shot out of a cannon, like the finale on the Fourth of July. I then decided to introduce another person, namely the speaker, whom I thought of as perhaps the mother of the "you," by giving expression to the speaker's attitude toward the delicate, unworldly "you":

4.
(First 9 lines as above)
You frighten me in that dress,
white gauze, as if you were going to stand,
a speechless bride, in the underground
fluorescence of alabaster and ice
until pale moths, blue-eyed like you,
settle on the back of your hand-

until I notice the orange belt,
your narrow lifeline.

   Still no solution. Next, I tried turning the syntax of the last 8 lines
around, so as to avoid having the orange belt come at you out of
nowhere in the end:

5.
(First 9 lines as above)
If it were not for the orange belt,
your narrow lifeline,
you would frighten me in that dress,
white gauze, as if you were going to stand,
a speechless bride, in the underground
fluorescence of alabaster and ice
until the pale moths, blue-eyed like you,
settle on the back of your hand.

   In the next two versions I played around with different possibilities
of solving this same problem of the too-neat reversal, by changing the
language somewhat and concentrating more on the mother's response
to the "you," but I finally had become fed up with the "belt" idea
altogether. What had seemed like such a lucky bit of inspiration had
come to seem like an annoying trick, and I dropped it entirely, leaving
my heroine standing there in the frozen underworld inviting the pale
moths, and ending with the expression of fear for her on the part of
the mother/speaker. I then left the end of the poem alone and made
a few small changes in the beginning and middle. For one thing, Emily
Dickinson was dropped; I realized it was much too cute. In the
beginning Emily Dickinson was important to me, in fact she had to be

there, since she appeared to me as the initial embodiment of
whiteness, the white Muse of the poem. But by now I had worked for
so long on other images that I had become removed from the initial
impulse and could let the invocation of Emily Dickinson go. By this
time I had completed 10 drafts of the poem, which was still called
"Going in White," and all my fiddling around had done nothing to
breathe life into it. It still had "exercise" written all over it:

10.
GOING IN WHITE

You love the moon for its frailty.
An albino rose, you call it,
precious in it aberration
to us tough ones, pink and red,
who are not harmed by the sun's
mustard and urine. You long for the world
pure, without the double distortion
of light filtered through air.

Your white dress frightens me--
gauze, as if you were going to enter,
a tearless bride, the fluorescence
of alabaster and ice
and wait for the palest moths,
blue-eyed like you,
to light on the back of your hand.

   The sequence of the sentences, especially in stanza 1, seemed
dutiful, and the syntax, even with the declarative clauses broken up,
stiff, mechanical and choppy: marching cadences, hardly appropriate
here. What's more, the poem was somehow unanchored and
incomplete. I pictured a reader asking, "Who is this 'you,' anyway?" I
began asking myself that question. I had reached an impasse, and I
knew that if I wanted to rescue the poem, I had to rethink the whole
formal premise. Or perhaps I should say, "think it through for the first
time," since originally I had let the poem grow from whatever images
came to me, undisciplined by thought.

At some point during the composing process I had thought of Whistler's painting, "The Little White Girl," also titled "Symphony in White." (There are actually four "White Girl" paintings; this one is the first and most famous.) Like all of Whistler's work, it is a study in exquisite, delicate tones and balances. A wistful young woman -- not really a little girl -- dressed all in white looks into a mirror over a mantel. The stance and the expression on her face make it appear that she is daydreaming, or lost in thought, rather than studying herself in the mirror. She is holding a Japanese fan and there are pink azalea blossoms in a vase on the floor next to her, both of which attenuate the delicacy of the feeling the painting conveys. Even though I had remembered this painting as I was working on the various drafts, I had resisted making any use of it because I had written a number of poems based on paintings over the years and I wanted to put that behind me. But at this stage I felt I had to use the painting as a point of reference, even though it had not been that when I began the poem. I knew I had to do more than simply change the title to something that would implicate Whistler, but I didn't yet know that I had to change the poem radically. Instead, I thought that its incompleteness could be made up for if I wrote two more sections based on other Whistler paintings, which would somehow relate to my white girl. I looked at books on Whistler and chose one of his "Nocturnes," a misty water scene with dark shades of color blending into each other and a faint harbor light or two. This seemed to me an extension of my moth image and could be seen as another manifestation of what the white girl represented. For the third section I used the famous portrait of his mother, in black, gray and white, which I thought might represent an aging version of the white girl. I wrote the three-part poem but wasn't happy with it. It didn't work well enough, probably because my heart wasn't really in it -- because it was merely a strategy to save the poem and my superimposition of a common denominator on all of these Whistler paintings was deliberate rather than spontaneous; it didn't arise out of a genuine revelation. It is one thing to discover, joyously and breathlessly, that all of an artist's paintings are different metaphors for the same vision; it is another to reason that this must be true and to set out to prove it. Besides, the poem had a different focus now -- it concentrated on Whistler's sensibility and had gotten away from whiteness as the emblem of a purity that stands in opposition

62

to robust life -- and I really didn't want to give that up.

I tried to go back to the beginning, this time with Whistler added. I still wanted to use the "White Girl" painting as an anchor but didn't want the poem to be <u>about</u> the painting. I figured I could come up with images that were in no way descriptive of the painting and still convey its sensibility, since I felt Whistler's and my way of seeing the quality of whiteness was close enough. The speaker was troubling me; I hadn't yet found the voice I needed. I decided to make her (I believe it is a female voice) a member of a group, an average, ordinary sort of person, who speaks of the white girl as an extraordinary person, someone "different," an outsider. Here is this version, by now the twelfth, with a changed title:

12.
IMPROVISATION ON A THEME BY WHISTLER

We line up on the side of the sun,
but she, the pale girl, loves
the albino moon, that precious
aberration. All summer
she wears white gauze to her ankles
and trains the pallid, chalky moths,
blue-eyed like her,
to light on her hair like petals.
Soul mates, she says. It is something to do
until the snow starts to fall
with the steady interior rhythm
only she can hear.
She stretches her arms, as if they were wounded,
toward the bandages of snow.
For once the world is hers,
not ours, in its perfect frailty.

The albino rose of the moon had simply become an albino moon, and the mustard and urine of the sun were gone. I had liked these metaphors in the beginning and had stuck with them for a long time, but the way the poem was going now, the images seemed to be drawing too much attention to themselves at the expense of the poem. Also I wanted the voice of the speaker to be natural; these

images were too fanciful to put into her mouth. I was pleased with
the snow/wound/bandage image, but the one about the moths,
retained from the pre-Whistler versions, didn't seem to work now. I
decided to use Whistler's mirror; it seemed appropriate. Somehow
the poem had moved closer and closer to an implication of narcissism.
Perhaps that was in my mind in the beginning, though I failed to
recognize it. Here is version 13, now cast in the past tense:

13.
We would line up on the side of the sun,
but she would choose the albino moon,
that precious aberration.
While we practiced Clementi,
She would play Chopin, always the nocturnes.
In summer she dressed in gauze
and turned her back to the window,
lost in the mirror, where her eyes,
two large blue moths, hung dreaming.
It was snow she was waiting for,
the first uncertain falling
with the interior hum
only she could hear.
She would stretch her arms, as if they were wounded,
toward the bandages of snow.
For a moment the world was hers
in its perfect frailty.

(It's only now, as I type this paper, that I realize Whistler's
"Nocturnes" which I examined in search of a three-part poem, have
surfaced here as Chopin's.)
I felt the poem was almost there. But the voice still struck me as
awkward. That's when I determined to let the poet be the speaker,
the general commentator not just on one particular girl, but on all
girls who are like this one: emotionally frail, daydreaming, for whom
life is forever crushing, brutal, too impure. The image of the mute
swan occurred to me and the fairy tale idea of transformation, in this
case reversed: of a human being who should have been a swan. As
the poet/commentator I could make such a statement more credibly
than my previous, fictional speaker. Draft 14 contains this image, and

the next three, which eliminate the piano playing and take care of minor changes in phrasing, keep it.

My final draft is 20. I am leaving the poem there for now, perhaps forever. The only bit of language left from the first draft is "the moon,/that precious aberration." I regret losing the frozen underworld, but at some point the poem stopped being about immobility and started to be about fragility. The moth image and the mother/daughter relationship are still here, though in a different guise, and I think the feeling toward the white girls of this world is not much different from the way it was in the beginning. The reversal is gone and I fancy, rightly or wrongly, that the ending does not box in the imagination to the extent it did in the "pre-Whistler" versions.

20.
AFTER WHISTLER

There are girls who should have been swans.
At birth their feathers are burned;
their human skins never fit.
When the other children
line up on the side of the sun,
they will choose the moon,
that precious aberration.
They are the daughters mothers
worry about. All summer,
dressed in gauze, they flicker
inside the shaded house,
drawn to the mirror, where their eyes,
two languid moths, hang dreaming.
It's winter they wait for, the first snowfall
with the steady interior hum
only they can hear:
they stretch their arms, as if they were wounded,
toward the bandages of snow.
Briefly, the world is theirs
in its perfect frailty.

AN INTERVIEW WITH LISEL MUELLER

NB: <u>How</u> <u>has</u> <u>being</u> <u>bilingual</u> <u>influenced</u> <u>your</u> <u>consciousness</u> <u>of</u>
<u>language?</u>
LM: We learn language by imitation; even people who don't know the grammar of their own language will speak it correctly if they hear it spoken correctly. Usage is another thing we just pick up. We don't think about our native language at all. But when you switch to another language, you are conscious of <u>everything</u>. You're conscious of the grammatical constructions, you're conscious of the phrasing, you're conscious of the idioms, you're conscious of each word -- what it means, how it is used in its various forms, its derivation, if there is a cognate in your own language, how it might differ -- all those things become so important. And metaphor is difficult at first. Like the popular song "Under a blanket of blue": I knew from the context it couldn't be a real blanket, but I didn't know it was the sky. And I didn't know "deep purple" meant nightfall. In German, I would have understood, any American would have understood...except we don't really listen to the words of popular songs in our native language. We hear those words, we say those words, and we never think about what they mean or whether they make any sense. I didn't in Germany, but coming here it became extremely important to be able to understand what every word meant. It's that kind of minute attention I think you have only with a language to which you're not native. Who knows, I might not have become a poet had this not happened to me.

My poetry is largely Germanic in the sense that I usually use strong, short words and not many latinates because they sound weaker to me -- conversational, essayistic. More and more latinates are coming into poetry because our whole speech is becoming more latinate. The younger people use words ending in -ion and so on much more freely than I would. Of course, that isn't unique to me. Look at Dylan Thomas or Hopkins or Roethke who almost exclusively used Germanic words, probably because they dealt with very elementary things. My poems too tend to deal with the elementary and I associate those strongly accented, strongly sounded Germanic words with elementary things. If you're going to discuss ideas, then latinates are appropriate; but I don't deal with them, at least not directly, in my poems.

NB: A number of people have commented that a fascination with language rather than an interest in ideas is the primary impetus for writing poetry.

LM: There are very few ideas worth talking about. Those ideas are good for all times, but unless a poet has a new way of dealing with those ideas, they become commonplace. And new insights, new connections, are inseparable from their language, which is why a paraphrase of a poem always sounds banal.

NB: Your later poetry seems more concerned with political and moral issues than your earlier poetry, or am I imagining things?

LM: No, I think that's true and I think the Vietnam War changed me. That's when I became angry about what was going on. Those were bad years for me, not in terms of my private life, but in terms of being involved in the shame and guilt and wrongness of this country. Like many of us at that time, I took it all very personally, and perhaps the history of Nazi Germany in the back of my mind made me feel involved with it. Also, my father was a historian much involved with contemporary history and perhaps the genes started to take.

NB: I also thought you implied that the large ethical and political questions post-war German writers had to confront enriched their work.

LM: World War I destroyed a lot of the assumptions, but lip service was still given to the nineteenth century virtues and values of decency and humanity and honesty. All of these assumptions were gone after World War II. They had all proved to be illusions. It was like starting from scratch for the writers who survived. They had a lot to catch up on. For about twenty years they had been virtually cut off from new European and American writings. There was a total physical leveling of much of Germany and thousands starved to death even after the war was over. Then there were all the revelations about the death camps and the whole monstrous history which had occurred as a result of the Nazis in Germany. So it was like starting from scratch both physically and spiritually. And it was important to find a new, untainted language. This is why a lot of the poetry seems very innovative as well as very stark -- almost stammering to come up with something new. And the novelists had a whole new subject. The Germans have had to come to grips with their history and they get their strength from writing about it.

67

NB: Your poem "The Fall of the Muse" seems critical of American poetry.

LM: It was written against the exhibitionism I thought was going on, not just in poetry - although the confessional poets are implicated in this. It was written after the death not only of Sylvia Plath, but of Judy Garland and Marilyn Monroe and biographers on talk shows were trying to top each other with intimate details about these people's lives. I felt moral outrage about this public suffering and this glamorizing of suffering. The temptation is to keep upping the ante and finally all you're left with is committing suicide.

NB: I think that some contemporary American writers romanticize neurosis and I tend to avoid teaching their work, although that may be a mistake.

LM: For obvious historical reasons American writers tend to focus on private psychic suffering, rather than the suffering brought on by social and political injustice. That kind of suffering is no less real than the suffering of a brutalized oppressed person, but it's less shareable. We feel that someone who really has it rough in the world...we feel that kind of suffering is more justified somehow than the suffering that goes on in so much of the more privileged part of society.

I don't know which makes the better writing because some of the novels that have come out of the more realistic, proletarian writing of the thirties and so on, haven't stood up either.

There is a problem with finding subject matter in our society, partly because there is a great bias among young writers against political writing. They don't want to write about political matters at all. Robert Bly and Denise Levertov have been attacked for their engagement in these issues -- the Vietnam War and nuclear disarmament and things of that sort. That seems to me a uniquely American and English tradition of disassociating writing from what goes on in the world because it's certainly not true of European writers and it's not true of South American writers. They're all involved in the politics of their country and they write about that; in countries where they can't write about it directly, like South Africa, Eastern Block countries, and Latin American countries, they write parables. They do it in an indirect way, but it's clearly understood.

NB: That certainly was a prejudice when I was in graduate school: bad writing is ideological and good writing is subtle and intricate.

I used to think it was intellectual elitism: the best writing is the most inaccessible.

LM: A friend once gave a poetry reading and after the reading someone came up to him said, "I enjoyed your poetry even though I can understand it." So, yes, there has been a lot of that. Luckily, I think that is changing.

NB: Some people have said that it's not good for literature to have so many writers sheltered by the academy.

LM: I don't know that it makes writing any less good, but I think it probably does make it more uniform. A lot of poets of our time sound very much alike; perhaps that's come out of the fact that most of us are teachers or writing students rather than working at Sears or driving a truck, or whatever. Writers used to have to support themselves in ways that had nothing to do with writing and this may make a difference in terms of struggling by yourself.

NB: You've written that you did exercises to teach yourself how to write poetry. Do you remember what they were?

LM: I did things like getting books on prosody out of the library and doing some of the things that were explained in there. For example, I would read about the villanelle and I would make myself write a villanelle. It was just a matter of reading books that explained the various forms and experimenting with them; I learned how they worked and tried to do some of them myself.

NB: Do you use anything like that with your students?

LM: It depends on the level of the students. Recently I've been teaching in a tutorial program and dealt largely with students who are already writers, graduate students. They know what they want to do and so I don't give them exercises. I let them write and then we discuss the work at hand. I suggest poets for them to read because I can see certain directions which I would like them to go in or certain things which I feel are not good about their work and I want them to read people they can learn from.

I've done some poetry in the schools and I give exercises with kids because you can't just say, "Sit down and write a poem." You have to give them specific instructions. Younger children are wonderful at metaphor. "Something is like something else" is a very simple way of explaining metaphor. "What does this remind you of?" "What is the color pink like for you?" Blue is an interesting color because some kids come up with all sad images and others come up with wonderful, exhilarating, blue images. Also, with natural phenomena, they're wonderful. I remember one kid saying, "Hail is like God dropping the ice cube out of his martini."

NB: Should I have my students read work they will understand even if it means they'll be reading Sandburg?

LM: It depends on the student. It depends on the age and level you're talking about. If you're teaching graduate students, no. Or if you have some ambitious young intellectual who will want to read only things that he or she can't understand...But high school students, yes. Give them something they can enjoy because most of them don't like poetry to begin with, or think they won't like it, so give them work that can somehow touch on their own experience, that's simple enough and yet respectable poetry. Don't give them Rod McKuen, don't give them Edgar Guest, but...Sandburg may not be the greatest poet we've ever had, but he was a poet. You need to start with something you don't feel bad about giving them, but which will engage their interest.

You have to grab them where they are. Then you may be able to get them to go on from there, but if you give them something that shuts them out at the beginning, you'll never get them.

NB: I was interested by your poem about giving your daughter a copy of Sister Carrie because a student once told me that the first time a book engrossed her was when we read Sister Carrie in class. The next term she got caught up in The Grapes of Wrath, but she thought the ending was too sad. I said, "Well, there's some hope that the Okies will get together." And she said, "Oh, I hope they do."

LM: Well, that's it. For young people the personal connection is very important. "Oh, I hope they do," it's as if it were happening to her own family. I have noticed that often someone who has read one of my books, a young student or someone who has come to a reading of mine, will come up and tell me about a poem they have liked, and it's almost always, "I know someone who has done this" or "I have felt this way" or "I've had this experience." They don't respond to it because it's a well-written poem; it's because there's something in the poem that touches them personally. That's always the beginning; the aesthetic thing comes later.

I was reading Sandburg my first year in this country, when I wasn't used to the language. At the same time I was reading Sandburg, I was taking my first high school English Literature course. I was reading Wordsworth and Keats and Gray and I couldn't do much with them.

They were simply too difficult for me; but Sandburg, I could read, I could understand, I could respond to. I knew that Keats and Wordsworth and Shelley and the rest were supposed to be much greater poets, but that didn't mean I really liked them.

NB: You've said that you wrote in free verse because you found "the echoes of the formal masters too strong" for your "incubating voice." Do your students have trouble with echoes?

LM: They have echoes, but they aren't those same echoes because they largely read contemporary poetry; so there'll be echoes of maybe Mark Strand or Galway Kinnell. It's never the traditionally formal poets because my students come from two generations in which they've not been taught metric poetry. A few years ago Donald Hall was teaching a short course in writing in iambic pentameter in the Goddard MFA Program, and students flocked to it. They found it extremely difficult and they found it fascinating: they were learning new things. And they found it very hard because they were used to speech rhythms; they were not used to hearing stressed and unstressed syllables. It was like learning to hear poetry in that way for the first time. So everything is turned around.

I've always, for example, liked to have my students read people like Richard Wilbur, who is an absolutely marvelous poet in whatever he does, but who, among other things, is very good with forms. And also someone like Marilyn Hacker who writes not only wonderful villanelles and sestinas and sonnets, but crowns of sonnets and double villanelles. She uses these very traditional forms, but uses extremely colloquial, idiomatic, contemporary language within these forms which I think is a beautiful and interesting combination. I like my students to read these people. It doesn't necessarily mean they write like them. It is hard for them to, say, write a sonnet that doesn't sound like tenth-rate Keats.

NB: If it's possible, I'd like you to explain this comment:"Once the tools, tricks and secrets of the trade become second nature, you lose the attention to technique which has served as a margin of safety. Suddenly you are nakedly exposed to the dangerous process of bringing a poem into existence."

LM: I meant that period between the time you know exactly what you do because you are doing an exercise and the time when you can trust your instinct and critical judgment enough that you don't feel totally at risk. It's like a child learning to walk. The child has held onto the furniture or the hands of grownups and then she lets go and for a little while, there'll be quite a few falls until, eventually, she stops falling and can walk by herself. There is a period like that and it's very troublesome for young writers. I certainly went through that for a number of years.

I get this in workshops where people who don't have much background in writing but a great deal of enthusiasm have no sense of whether the poem works and also whether it communicates its ideas to an outside reader. Often they're very good at criticizing poems by other people but they can't do it to their own poems. I'll talk to them about a specific poem and try to help them see some of the problems and they will say, "Well, you've been very helpful and now I see what you mean, but why can't I do this myself?" There's no way except the experience of writing and writing and revising, going back, looking at your old poems. There comes a day when you can do it, when the flaws jump out at you.

NB: It sounds as though that middle period is a time when the person hasn't really established a center for his or her work.

LM: That's true, but it's also a matter of learning the craft. Most young writers are very awkward in their language. Even if there's a great deal of talent there, a great deal of energy, the phrasing is usually not smooth yet, not lapidary enough. It's also proportion and pace and transition, how to get from here to there, all those technical things which you have to learn by feel on your own. You develop your own voice, your own language, and that takes time.

NB: Can having other people react to their work speed that process up?

LM: I think it can and that's why workshops are so valuable and such a shortcut for writers. It's something I didn't have when I started to write. Students in workshops get that immediate response from a teacher who's an experienced writer and from their fellow students.

NB: If someone couldn't go to a workshop, what would you suggest they do to teach themselves?

LM: Read the best poets - all the good poets of their time as well as the older literature. We learn to write by imitation largely, just as we learn to speak and walk by imitation. I think most teachers --
probably all poets teaching -- would agree that they're merely helping along and that the reading is the primary thing. The teacher can be very valuable in helping direct students to what to read. One of the

72

good things about the Goddard program, now at Warren Wilson College, is that each program is individually made up for a particular student, and that it requires a lot of reading. It encourages not only reading poetry and criticism and fiction, but also reading outside of literature -- reading about science or architecture or psychology -- other subjects that could feed into your poetry as subject matter and enrich your sense of the world. Sometimes young writers don't want to read anything outside of literature and that's a very small part...The world is rich. Any writer is a better writer the less insulated he or she is.

Reading widely makes you a livelier, richer person and that would feed into your writing. It's probably more important for novelists than for poets because they deal with social reality whereas poets deal largely with their inner world or how their inner world relates to the outer world, but I think it enriches the whole <u>context</u> in which you write. W.H. Auden, for example, regretted very much that he didn't know more about nature, especially botany and zoology, than he did. He felt it would have helped his poetry a great deal if he had been able to use that area of knowledge in a natural way, the way, for example, Roethke did.

Even being a good writer, but <u>definitely</u> being a <u>great</u> writer, demands a great deal of understanding and knowledge of the world. It doesn't necessarily mean a formal education, but it does involve curiosity. That's what we feel in Tolstoy and Thomas Mann and Flaubert and the great poets like Yeats or Keats. One has that sense that they were interested in a very large universe.

I'm partial to history. To me a sense of what has gone on in the past is very important to one's view of the world. Because that is my bias in writing poetry, I look at what is going on right now in my life and the life of people around me not as divorced from everything that has gone before, but in the context of the past and of what may come in the future. Now that's not everyone's bias. For some people it may be nature. Everything related to the seasonal, to the rejuvenation of nature, or perhaps it relates to landscape. There are poets whose whole world of inner experience is articulated in terms of natural images; it's as if the landscape or the weather is as metaphor always for what is going on inside them. There are many different possibilities.

I don't mean a writer can't be a wonderful writer and have a highly concentrated vision. There are writers who are obsessed by one thing and that one thing is expressed over and over and wonderfully. It's the hedgehog and the fox idea. The hedgehog is the one who burrows inside; Kafka is a typical hedgehog. He had this one idiosyncratic vision of everything, and it was such a <u>powerful</u> vision...perhaps if he had dissipated it, it would not have been so powerful. And then there are the foxes like Tolstoy. But I think even for the obsessive ones, knowing as much as possible is valuable and a joy.

NB: <u>Do</u> <u>you</u> <u>get</u> <u>anything</u> <u>from</u> <u>teaching?</u>

LM: I've enjoyed the method of tutorial teaching very much. I like working with one person at a time, being able to relate to his or her particular needs, and see the direction they're going in. I can't really help someone without understanding their poetry and that means trying to get into that person's mind.

I like the exchange of talking about literature. Having to do it by mail, as I've had to do with my students, is laborious, but it makes you think hard about everything you say because it's down on paper and there are so many more possibilities of misunderstanding. It's taught me to think abut things more clearly than I would otherwise. It's also forced me to read a lot more because I've had to keep up with the students' reading and they want to read a lot of things I haven't read. It's been stimulating for me. There is the pleasure of the intellectual-literary exchange, but also of seeing someone develop and maybe having a share in guiding their development.

(Interview conducted by Nancy Bunge)